Also translated by Sylvain Gallais and Cynthia Hogue

Joan Darc, by Nathalie Quintane

Fortino Sámano (The Overflowing of the Poem)
by Virginie Lalucq and Jean-Luc Nancy

DISTANTLY

DISTANTLY

Nicole Brossard

Translated by Sylvain Gallais and
Cynthia Hogue

OMNIDAWN PUBLISHING
OAKLAND, CALIFORNIA
2022

Cover art: Cynthia E. Miller, born 1953, "New York, April, 2009," Acrylic paint with chalk pastels and oil paintstick on canvas 32" x 52" Photographed by Tim Fuller, Private Collection Cemillerart.com

Typefaces: Garamond Premier Pro and Briem Script Std

Cover design by Adam Bohannon
Interior design by Ken Keegan

Library of Congress Cataloging-in-Publication Data

Names: Brossard, Nicole, author. | Gallais, Sylvain, translator. | Hogue, Cynthia, translator. | Brossard, Nicole. Lointaines. | Brossard, Nicole. Lointaines. English. Title: Distantly / Nicole Brossard ; translated by Sylvain Gallais and Cynthia Hogue.
Description: Oakland, California : Omnidawn Publishing, 2022. | French and English. | Summary: "This bilingual edition of Nicole Brossard's exuberantly lyrical collection, entitled in English Distantly, is a sequence of lush, taut cityscapes. Known for her elliptical and materially grounded poetics, Brossard creates in Distantly an intimate series drawn loosely from urban experience. The poems are linked by their city settings, drawn from a woman's observations, emotions, perceptions, and dreams as she wanders the streets of her world. The cities of the individual poem titles are evocatively conjured rather than realistically described. Taken together, these poems distill postmodern urban life through their sharp flash sketches of cultural and gendered histories of violence and beauty, personal and shared struggles for survival and intimacy. Distantly expresses a redolently postmodern sensibility, at once utopian and real"—Provided by publisher.
Identifiers: LCCN 2022007186 | ISBN 9781632431011 (trade paperback)
Subjects: LCSH: Brossard, Nicole--Translations into English. | Cities and towns--Poetry. | LCGFT: Poetry.
Classification: LCC PQ3919.2.B75 L6513 2022 | DDC 841/.914--dc23/eng/20220218
LC record available at https://lccn.loc.gov/2022007186

Published by Omnidawn Publishing, Oakland, California
www.omnidawn.com   (510) 237-5472
10 9 8 7 6 5 4 3 2 1
ISBN: 978-1-63243-101-1

Table Of Contents

Acknowledgments

Gratitude goes to the stalwart editors at Omnidawn, Rusty Morrison and Ken Keegan, for their abiding commitment to this translation through thick and thin, and to the editors of the following journals for publishing selected translations from *Lointaines* by Nicole Brossard, sometimes in earlier versions and sometimes in special features:

Arkansas International: "Cities with or without war," "Cities where my face returns," "Cities really" (three sections), "Cities with a thought that returns."

Hayden's Ferry Review: "Cities really" (one section), "Echoing cities," "Cities with faces," "Cities with their dead," "Cities without water."

Los Angeles Review: "Cities with their name," "City with its name (two sections)," "Cities really" (one section), "Cities after misfortunes," "Cities with a face."

On the Seawall: "Nicole Brossard: author's note," "Cities with their name" (two sections), "Cities where I haven't been," "Cities really" (one section), "Cities with their masks."

Persimmon Tree: "Cities with their oysters."

Two Lines: "Cities with their fools for God," "Cities really" (two sections), "Cities with a face" (two sections).

"Cities really" (two sections) and "Cities without names" (two sections) were featured in an online exclusive in *Two Lines*.

A funded faculty leave from the Department of English at Arizona State University (ASU) helped Cynthia Hogue to advance these translations. In addition, faculty development funding from the Maxine and Jonathan Marshall Endowment supported the book's progress. The translators are grateful for the precious gifts of time and money. The translators also wish to thank the following individuals who helped at various stages: Paul Morris, Alberto Rios, Cole Swensen, Tim Schaffner, Eleanor Wilner, Joan Larkin, Aliki Barnstone, Christopher Burawa, and to Hogue's 2014 graduate class in Literary Translation, a big shout out for your beautiful work and inspiring discussions about the art of translation!

Over the years of working on the translation of *Lointaines*, we consulted Nicole Brossard many times (although unfortunately, not in person). She has been ever-encouraging, gracious and helpful. We are profoundly grateful to her for being a guiding presence and resource throughout, as we grew deeply to appreciate these exquisite poems. We hope to have conveyed something of their lyric beauty and poetic importance in English. We also extend our thanks to Brossard's generous editor at Éditions Caractères, Nicole Gdalia, who readily extended us permission to publish our individual translations along the way, and then the full-length English translation.

It's worth noting that finalizing the agreement to publish this bilingual edition was full of high drama and challenges. Our publisher was greatly impacted by the tragic California fires of both 2019 and 2020. Then the world shut down in the pandemic. We (sheltering in Tucson) completed the final revision of *Distantly*, and during that intense time, deepened our appreciation of Brossard's attentiveness to the emotional and ecological surroundings of each city about which she writes, to earth's marginalized populations, to the lived lives of women who love women, and as is clearer now than two years ago, to the fate of earth itself.

Translators' Foreword

Renowned in contemporary Francophone literature, Nicole Brossard has been in the forefront of the dynamic Québécois feminist, lesbian and avant-garde writing communities, devoting herself to writing as both vocation and avocation since the 1970s. She has produced over fifty volumes of poetry, fiction, and nonfiction, authored a play, directed a film, and edited a number of anthologies and special journal issues. Known for the sensual intensity of her work and the originality of her poetics, she is now recognized as one of the most significant Francophone writers of her generation. Recipient of many honors, including the W. O. Mitchell Award and the Molson Prize from the Canada Council, she received the prestigious Lifetime Recognition Award for 2019 from the Griffin Trust.

Although a number of major works have been translated over the past four decades, Brossard is prolific, and more translations are in order. Notably, to address this concern, *Mauve Desert* (originally published in translation in 1990) was reissued in 2006. Several translations by Robert Majzels and Erin Mouré—*Installations, Museum of Bone and Water,* and *Notebook of Roses and Civilization*—were published within the last fifteen years, as was a selection of poems, *Mobility of Light,* edited by Louise Forsyth. *Selections: Nicole Brossard,* published in 2010, included poems selected by Brossard herself and translated by prominent poet-translators, a selection of Brossard's most significant poetics essays and interviews, and a superb critical introduction by Jennifer Moxley.[1] More recently, Coach House Press published *Avant Desire* in 2020, a compendium reader of Brossard's poetry over the course of her career, edited by Sina Queyras et al. We hope that our bilingual edition of Brossard's elliptically engaged series of linked poems, *Lointaines*—translated as *Distantly* into English for the first time—will contribute to the growing Brossard canon in English.

Brossard's work is at once exuberantly lyrical and materially (politically) grounded. Moxley describes her poetry as "effortlessly

---

[1] Nicole Brossard, *Selections: Nicole Brossard,* edited, and with an introduction by Jennifer Moxley (Berkeley: U of CA P, 2010). Hereafter cited parenthetically in text as NB, followed by the page number.

reunit[ing] the aesthetic and the political, updating the meaning of both as it does so" (*NB*, 2). As Brossard explains in "Poetic Politics," she creates this union by rooting her writing in the body (*corps*), which serves as a "channel" for the flow of its energy, drives, and desires into language, the text (*texte*). She quips that the punning phrase "*Le Cortex exubérant*" encapsulates her lifelong "obsession" with embodied language. The body "needs language to process energy into social meaning" (*NB*, 180). To be *socially* meaningful, however, language must be read. If a "text shows its politics" in "the writing," as Brossard theorizes in "Poetic Politics," it is in the reading of the text that it becomes "political" (*NB*, 186).

Brossard is careful to situate her writing and creative process in relation to the language of power (the Patriarchy). It matters that her language is produced by a subject writing as a woman, a lesbian and feminist, a mother and a humanist. Influenced by French poststructuralist and feminist theory, she defines her poetic as making "a space for the unthought" (*NB*, 190). That is, she is *creating* space in her work for all who have never been accorded it in the arena of "social meaning" (the Symbolic), including populations of the marginalized. She observes in the world so much that has been unseen and inaudible—women's desires, dreams, experiences, memories—because never *made space for*, thus remaining unarticulated, *unthought*.

Brossard terms this imaginary, as Lynette Hunter has incisively analyzed, the *inédit*: literally, the unpublished, but conceptually, a term for the "not-yet-said." [2] As Hunter explains, the process of articulation "breathes the material reality of the *inédit* into sound and resonance"—that is, into poetry—making it "possible for the powerful to hear those erased from or marginal to power" (Hunter, 237). Brossard is concerned to create by means of her writing a space for the articulation of what we have chosen to translate as "the unscribed," the *inédit,* in Brossard's sense of the

---

[2] Lynette Hunter, "The *Inédit* in Writing by Nicole Brossard: *Breathing the Skin of Language,*" in *Nicole Brossard: Essays on Her Works,* ed. Louise H. Forsyth (Toronto: Guernica, 2005), 209-38. Hereafter cited parenthetically in text as Hunter, followed by the page number.

term, signifying "a new space" for "new materials to be taken into account about life and its meanings" (*NB*, 188). For Brossard, such writing helps us to expand our knowledge and transform our vision.

Brossard does not write in autobiographical or narrative detail, although it is clear that the speaker of her poems in *Distantly* is writing out of the specificity of lived experience, from the sensual impressions and responsive articulations of a particular embodied life. The poems are linked through the theme of life in cities (every poem title begins with "cities" or "city"). The poems are gorgeously lyrical in style, and the series as a whole is based loosely on the observations, emotions, perceptions, and dreams of a female speaking subject. The cities of the individual poems are not described realistically, although they are full of reality-based details. Taken together, the poems make up a series of evocative distillations rather than "thick" descriptions of postmodern urban life, with a sharp awareness, hovering at the edges, of social, cultural and gendered histories of violence and beauty, personal and political struggles for survival and intimacy.

Thus, the cities in Brossard's poems are not "Our Towns," but unfamiliar, uncanny. They may at first seem simply surreal, but in them dwell survivors of "misfortunes" who respond sorrowfully to the fact of "saris on fire" (with girls tragically still in them), urban landscapes with their "gleaming debris" and "bridges, ghats, / rivers in a time of peace and torture"—words which have clearly been written in the first violent decade of the twenty-first century. The lack of specificity gestures not only toward a transmuted, socially meaningful context, but also to a more intimate, transpersonal quest "to meet the horizon the day after the horizon." As Brossard writes in her author's note, which prefaces the collection, "*Distantly* is probably the best translation I can offer for the words horizon and breakers, each gathering momentum and marking a space far beyond elsewhere and ardor." Moxley understands Brossard as both an idealist and pragmatist, which makes it "possible not only to imagine a better future, but also to more easily love and breathe right now" (*NB*, 15). Finally, the poems in *Distantly* express an exquisitely postmodern sensibility, at once utopian and real.

Author's Note

depuis toujours je recommence mes villes,
la même, une autre encore et son pluriel
avec un goût de fruits de mer, une toile de
Caravage, un pont suspendu, un goût de
langue étrangère qui m'oblige à respirer
dans la lenteur et la vitesse de mon autre
corps de vertige

Lointaines est sans doute la meilleure
traduction que je puisse offrir pour les
mots horizon et déferlante, chacun prenant
son élan et traçant son espace bien au-delà
de l'ailleurs et de l'ardeur. *Lointaines*, c'est aussi
quand je pense à toi, aux fontaines et au verbe
être

n.b.

always I take up my cities again,

the same one, or another and its plural

with a taste of seafood, a painting by

Caravaggio, a suspension bridge, taste of

a foreign tongue that forces me to breathe

in the slowness and speed of my other

body of vertigo

Distantly is doubtless the best

translation I can offer for the words

horizon and breakers, each gathering

momentum and marking a space far beyond

elsewhere and ardor. *Distantly* is also when

I'm thinking of you, of fountains and the verb

to be

n. b.

Distantly

Nicole Brossard

Translated by Sylvain Gallais and Cynthia Hogue

Villes avec un visage

les jours de présence à bout portant
dans la tête, c'est
la disparition des arbres
des ponts des autres passant
entre les combats de rue, les incendies

peu à peu on dira
décompte d'éternité
traversant les visages

Cities with a face

days of presence at point-blank
to the head, this
is the disappearance of trees
of bridges of others passing
among the street fights, the fires

little by little we'll say
the count of eternity's
crossing our faces

oui, je m'habitue à l'idée de l'aura

à l'écran des corps restés là comme une empreinte

au coin d'une rue, sous la constellation du chien

dans les pensées je m'habitue à l'absence

yes, I'm used to the idea of the aura

to the outline of bodies lingering like a trace

on street corners, under the dog star constellation

in my mind I'm used to absence

Villes réellement

villes effleurées d'où tu regardes
les petits bras d'Isabelle Huppert
quand elle récite
les mots de Sarah Kane
villes effleurées où quelqu'un demande
parfois si ça soulage un incendie
ou peut-être aussi un tatouage

Cities really

cities stroked where you watch
the slender arms of Isabelle Huppert
as she recites
the words of Sarah Kane
cities stroked where someone asks
if sometimes a fire is soothing
as well as perhaps a tattoo

au loin avec leurs cernes jaunes

ou de près tap tap de quotidien d'ennui

clapotis de fontaine féerie néons de nuit

villes avec leurs grands tiroirs verticaux

les Martini 4 olives et murmures

au loin villes flirtées dans le flou des civilisations

nos mains entre joies souples

parois de miroir et de mélancolie

l'électricité qui chute dans nos cheveux

in the distance with their yellow circles

or the closer tap tap of daily boredom

lap of fountain fairy-neons of night

cities with their tall vertical cabinets

Martinis 4 olives and murmurs

in the distance cities wooed by the haze of civilizations

our hands between supple joys

walls of mirrors and melancholy

electricity which falls through our hair

villes dans l'eau jusqu'à la ceinture

jusqu'à la destruction lente et molle du matin

ton sourire qui remonte à si loin

puis émerger sera

un verbe utile et strident

cities in water up to their waist

until the morning's slow and languid destruction

your smile stretching so far back

that to emerge will be

a useful and strident verb

villes suspendues au-dessus des heures

avec leurs paupières de renaissance

leurs ficelles pour guérir

repoussant le chien le singe

dans les musées

frôlant paumes et poings pour camoufler

l'odeur de peur, l'instinct quotidien

cities suspended above the hours

with their renaissance eyelids

their secrets for healing

pushing the dog the monkey

into museums

brushing palm and fist to cover

the odor of fear, the daily instinct

villes du très grand Nord

où j'apprends à toucher

la matière grise des bêtes

leur peau sur les comptoirs

à essuyer le sang sur mes mains

pour saluer qui vient

de l'horizon turquoise des glaciers

avec une soif et un appétit qui tissent un lien

entre la tendresse et le froid

cities in the far North

where I've learned to touch

the gray matter of animals

their skins on counters

to wipe the blood off my hands

so I can greet anyone who drops by

from the turquoise horizon of glaciers

with a thirst and hunger forging a link

between tenderness and frost

Villes avec leur nom

Florence Venise ou Bologne
quelqu'un aura cru
à l'or à la soie sous les doigts
paume heureuse effleurant
le marbre et le granite rose
tant d'ivresse devant la planète ronde
l'odeur des premières dissections
le sang qui coule dans un corps inédit

Cities with their name

Florence Venice or Bologna
someone will have believed
in gold in silk to the touch
palm happy stroking
the marble and rose granite
such delirium before this round planet
odor of first dissections
blood pooling in an unscribed body

au loin Prague, le pont le château

l'heure dans l'horloge

l'horloge dans l'histoire

le cimetière juif au tournant

Skopje, Istanbul autres alphabets

commerce d'heures et d'épices comme rivière

rouge safran pulsant dans le temps

in the distance Prague, the bridge the castle

the time on the clock tower

the clock tower in history

the Jewish cemetery at the corner

Skopje, Istanbul other alphabets

commerce of hours and spices like a river

red saffron pulsing with time

de face et de dos avoir un sexe

des ongles d'esclaves

pas de lit ni lavabo

Storyville ou Benin City

il se peut que nous n'ayons pas à décrire

seulement à replacer la peur

à l'endroit où nous l'avons trouvée

from front and from back to have a sex

from the nails of slaves

no bed or basin

Storyville or Benin City

it could be that we don't have to describe

but only to return fear

to the place where we found it

Villes réellement

dans le vif des gestes
villes avec uppercuts swings et hijabs
rap qui nique les mères
comme on noie les chats
villes rubans où tu apprends à dire
je au bon moment quand chacun pour soi
avec son visage de courte paille
roule poings serrés entre les métaphores

Cities really

in the heart of gestures
cities with uppercuts swings and hijabs
rap that fucks mothers
like drowning cats
ribbon cities where you learn to say I
at a moment when everyone's out for themselves
with a look of getting the short straw
clenched fists packed between metaphors

villes avec leurs vieilles piles de malheurs

vacillantes

entre mémoire et marées d'emportements virtuels

tellement

que noir et très gris de poussière et de cris font

dans ma bouche une érosion

de vie qui ne se partage pas

cities with their old piles of misfortunes

vacillant

between memory and tides of virtual passion

so much

that black and very gray with dust and cries make

in my mouth an erosion

of life that can't be shared

Villes d'écho

villes avec le mot corail
pour observer par en dedans
l'ombre des veines

au galop avec l'écume et l'écho
des mots et mirages dans nos bouches
je voudrais revient
si souvent que d'ardeur
l'horizon tressaille
surprend en petites tendresses se répète
blessures à tout coup

Cities of echo

cities with the word coral
so as to observe from the inside
the shadow of veins

at a gallop with foam and echo
of words and mirage in our mouths
I would like
returns so often that with ardor
the horizon trembles
surprises with small tendernesses it repeats
hurts every time

Villes où je ne fus pas

Bagdad Vaduz et Samarcande
où je ne fus pas
autre qu'en lisant
me déplaçant de la forêt au désert halogène
rêvant de ne rien
massacrer à force de répétition
déterrant ici une parure d'amour, un bras
là-bas une impossible notion de futur
et toujours la voix de B. Heidsieck
qui exhume un à un les peuples
les recouvre d'une immensité si grande
que je suis déjà dans la disparition

Cities where I haven't been

Bagdad Vaduz and Samarkand
where I haven't been
except by reading
moving from forest to halogen desert
dreaming of massacring
nothing by force of repetition
unearthing here love's lure, an arm
there an impossible notion of the future
and always the voice of B. Heidsieck
which exhumes one by one all peoples
covering them with so large an immensity
I'm already part of the disappearance

Villes avec un visage

tant d'idées reçues comme un gouffre
dans mes muscles
tout près on dit que c'est toi mais c'est nous
avec une pensée pour les ponts, les ghâts
les fleuves en temps de paix et de torture

une caresse sur le lobe de l'oreille
villes faites pour nous embrouiller l'âme
dans la beauté bleue du rêve

Cities with a face

so many received ideas like a chasm
in my muscles
up close I say it's you but it's us
thinking of bridges, ghats
rivers in times of peace and torture

a caress on the earlobe
cities made to confuse our souls
in the blue beauty of dreams

Ville avec son nom

à l'embouchure de toutes les arrivées
de chaque adieu pour le mieux
bras tendu flamboyant de *freedom*
ou trompette coruscante de Miles Davis
ville au cœur loquace quand la civilisation
tourne à vide hurle ou s'effondre
nomade d'exil et d'opulence
New York et son eau d'Atlantide
square de performance et de traduction
New York chrono

City with its name

at the mouth of all arrivals
of each farewell for the best
outstretched arms flamboyant with *freedom*
or coruscating trumpet of Miles Davis
city of loquacious heart when civilization
spinning its wheels howls or collapses
nomad of exile and opulence
New York and its waters of Atlantis
square of performance and translation
New York chrono

Villes avec leurs masques

c'est seulement quand le mot vient

sous la langue installer samba et minuetto

que favelas et Grand canal

masques et regards du fin fond de l'âme des morts

font

corps à corps d'intrigues et de défis

cela tu le sais en regardant les colliers, les nuques

l'une la noire, l'une la blanche

la variété des délires

selon l'idée que tu te fais de la liberté

Cities with their masks

it's only when the word comes

under the tongue bringing samba and minuet

that favelas and Grand Canal

masks and looks from the very depths of the souls of the dead

make

body to body intrigue and defiance

this you know seeing the necklaces, the napes

one black, one white

the variety of deliriums

depending on your idea of liberty

Villes avec leurs morts

pas de cimetières vraiment que des morts
des mots pour ne pas dire, pas prénoms, pas son nom
pas encore un malheur, petits pas qui glacent
à chaque année je marche dans une ville neuve
avec des mots des os des cheveux des lunettes
je marche avec quelqu'un qui a écrit un livre
« puis s'en est allé sur la pointe des pieds* »
retrouver l'horizon le lendemain de l'horizon

*Anne Hébert

Cities with their dead

no cemeteries really only the dead
words not to say, no first names no names
not misfortune yet, small steps that freeze
each year I walk through a new city
with words with bones with hair with glasses
I walk with someone who wrote a book
"then took leave on tiptoes*"
to meet the horizon the day after the horizon

* Anne Hébert

Villes sans eau

à l'heure des désirs brefs du matin
une goutte d'eau et sa lumière
plus tard pour contrer la poussière
il a fallu chercher l'herbe le buisson
une quelconque trace
du temps fluide et incliné à l'heure
qui assoiffe en nous le songe

Cities without water

at the hour of morning's brief desires
a drop of water and its light
later to counter the dust
we had to search for the herb the bush
some trace
of liquid and gradient time at the hour
which parches the dream inside us

Villes avec leurs fous de dieu

cette fois-ci je compte les mains, les pieds,

les langues, les tuniques, les cailloux

les têtes, les barbes

les calottes, les voiles, les châles,

je ne compte pas les vertiges

les ablutions les miracles

les coups de fouet,

dans les hauts parleurs

des dizaines de crachats de mots, un feu si grand

qu'il faut de l'eau sur le front, les pieds,

je compte les yeux, les doigts,

je compte jusqu'à la poussière

je compte jusqu'à l'enfance

Cities with their fools for God

this time I count the hands, the feet,

the tongues, the tunics, the pebbles

the heads, the beards

the skullcaps, the veils, the scarves,

I do not count the vertigos

the ablutions the miracles

the whiplashes

in the loudspeakers

the dozens of spat-out words, such a big fire

that water must be splashed on brow, on feet,

I count the eyes, the fingers,

I count until the dust

I count until childhood

Villes avec une pensée qui revient

je m'enflamme parfois
à cause de la population
n'importe qui peut
désormais compter les cadavres
avec leurs noms ou sans leur visage
les nuits quand c'est trop noir
je m'enflamme au moins une fois
dans une ville
parfois c'est deux la même nuit
et je ne dis jamais adieu

Cities with a thought that returns

sometimes I'm on fire

because of the population

anyone can

from now on count the corpses

with their names or without their faces

nights when it's too dark

I'm on fire at least once

in a city

sometimes twice in the same night

and I never say farewell

Villes avec leurs huîtres

sel aux joues, j'aime

cette saveur de matière intime qui nourrit

les pensées, vin, épaules nues des nuits d'été

à Sète, à Sitges et dans toute la vallée de Memramcook

la tête en amont du silence

je sais m'imprégner de l'huître et de son sel de claire

Cities with their oysters

salt on my lips, I love
this savor of intimate matter that nourishes
thought, wine, the naked shoulders of summer nights
in Sète, in Sitges and the whole valley of Memramcook
my head upstream of silence
I know how to relish the oyster and its salt-fresh *claire*

Villes réellement

quand le froid taille dans les arbres
de petites agglomérations de sens
si tu apprends à toucher
facilement l'épaule de quelqu'un
pour changer l'avenir
touche

Cities really

when the cold carves in the trees
small agglomerations of meaning
if you learn how to touch
someone's shoulder easily
to change the future
touch

grises roses ou sans feu

villes balayées par les aubes

survolées comme champs de mines

avec réponses au loin enfouies

on dirait douleur fantôme entourée

des pétales bleus d'un après-midi

villes au présent sans dire adieu

rose grays or no fire

cities swept by the dawns

flown over like mine fields

with answers buried far away

we could say a phantom pain circled

by blue petals on an afternoon

cities at present not saying farewell

Villes après le malheur

quand le silence inonde
la lumière avant et après le malheur
villes avec du vent dans les cheveux
puisque tu aimes en marchant
sur les ponts bien sentir l'eau de torrent
rouler dans le temps comme en la poitrine
puis tu les aperçois revenant de loin
Paul Celan et Virginia Woolf
dans leur élan de grande marche

Cities after misfortune

when silence inundates
light before and after misfortune
cities with the wind in your hair
because you love to walk over bridges
feeling deeply the torrent's waters
rolling through time like your ribcage
then you glimpse returning from afar
Paul Celan and Virginia Woolf
in the wake of their long walk

Villes réellement

villes d'abîme avec leurs racines

de jadis au présent

couteaux longs et cous fins de fillettes

incendies de saris

villes sans recommencement de lumière

avec leurs entassements de femmes et de cailloux

Cities really

abysmal cities with their roots

from ages ago to the present

long knives and slender necks of young girls

saris on fire

cities without resumption of light

with their mounds of women and stones

Villes avec un visage

parce qu'il vaut mieux soupirer

au-delà des croyances et plus loin

la solitude encore

voici que tu la déploies

devant toi comme quelqu'un qui veut

toute la mer pour soi

son infaillible lumière d'emportement

Cities with a face

because it's better to sigh
beyond beliefs and further
still the solitude
here you spread arms wide
before you like someone who wants
the whole sea for herself
its infallible light of passion

sans avoir peur de la peur

ni du vent méticuleux

qui annule au passage les pensées dociles

villes couchées en chien de fusil

comme le font un jour les civilisations

puisque nous rêvons en continu

d'un autre rêve déjà un autre rêve confondu

aux nuits de déluge et de chagrin

with no fear of fear

or of the meticulous wind

which in passing cancels docile thoughts

cities lie all curled up

as do sooner or later civilizations

because we dream continuously

of another dream already confused with another dream

of nights of deluge and grief

Villes sans nom

quand la réalité déferle
tu dis villes sans nom
arbres soudain trop grands
pour ta mémoire d'enfance
dans ton regard toujours
un présent d'absence déjoue
tes intentions les plus fleuves

Cities without names

when reality surges
you say cities without names
trees suddenly too tall
for your memory of childhood
in your eyes always
a presence of absence thwarts
your intentions those great rivers

villes parce qu'on est sincère

avec nos ombres de nouveau monde

enfoncées dans le temps et le sentiment

villes pleines de nos odeurs de fin du monde

avec leurs bûchers, leurs veuves

leurs ponts passages et fleuves d'encre

cities because we're honest

with our shadows of a new world

buried deep in time and feeling

cities filled with our odors at world's end

with its pyres, its widows,

its bridges passages and rivers of ink

villes quand quelqu'un te bouscule

dit *sorry sorrow* à cause du bruit et de la pluie

s'empare à bras-le-corps

d'une mélodie pour soulever le présent

son parfum fort de changement qui fascine

tous les matins quand même

tu l'aimes bras ballants l'humanité

sans oxygène au milieu de ses débris rutilant

cities when someone shoves you

says *sorry sorrow* because of the din and the rain

wraps arms around

a melody to lift up the present

the strong perfume of change which fascinates

you every morning anyway

you love humanity with helpless arms

without oxygen in the middle of its gleaming debris

Villes avec ou sans la guerre

villes avec soldats debout
toujours effrayants entre flammes
et monuments, soldat devant homme fou
homme fou devant soldat
d'un tir d'un coup tranchant
comme si la terre était peuplée de chèvres

alors vite villes traversées en dix minutes
comme Moose Jaw et Regina
dans la plaine en touchant l'aube de l'index

Cities with or without war

cities with standing soldiers
always frightening among flames
and monuments, a soldier facing a madman
a madman facing a soldier
with a shot a sharp blow
as if earth were peopled by goats

then quickly cities crossed in ten minutes
like Moose Jaw and Regina
on the plain your finger touching dawn

villes où l'on est toujours près

de quelqu'un debout entre les archives

et le visage de sa mère à rattraper

d'un coup de mémoire et d'horizon

cities where you're always close
to someone standing among the archives
to recapture her mother's face
in a stroke of memory and horizon

Ville avec son nom

un seul hurlement de néons

milliers de jetons et de passants

spectateurs de cirque et de hasard

écorchés vifs d'ardeur

dans le désert si beau si rouge

Las Vegas ses dés et tapis de paris

sa tour Eiffel, ses gondoles ce ciel de Venise

si bleu si faux

pétale comestible déployé comme un envers de liberté

strip de futur, surveillance marchande

City with its name

a single neon howl

thousands of tokens and passers-by

spectators of circus and chance

flayed alive by ardor

in the desert so beautiful so red

Las Vegas its dice and baize of bets

its Eiffel tower, its gondolas this sky of Venice

so blue so fake

edible petal spread like the reverse of liberty

strip of future, marketing surveillance

Villes avec mon visage qui revient

villes avec espoir dans la mire des sanglots
pensons-nous que l'aube est un mot
ou avons-nous dit par erreur *tengo sueño*
ce matin-là dans une ville d'Amérique
sourire sève au-delà de tous les calendriers
je respire lentement
une vie de mots fresques :
femmes lovées dans une joie d'errance et d'infini

Cities where my face returns

cities with hope in the crosshairs of sobs
do we think that dawn is a word
or have we said by accident *tengo sueño*
this very morning in a city in America
to smile sap beyond all schedules
I breathe slowly
a life of frescoed words :
women wrapped in the joy of wandering and infinity

Author Biography

Nicole Brossard has been in the
vanguard of the dynamic Fran-
cophone Canadian feminist and
avant-garde writing community for
over four decades. For her writing,
she has twice received the Grand
Prix du festival international de
poésie, among many other honors.
She has published over fifty books,
including *Ardeur, Lointaines, Piano
blanc, Lumière, fragment d'envers,*
and a book on translation, *Et me voici soudain en train de refaire
le monde.* In 2019, she was awarded the Lifetime Recognition
Award from The Griffin Trust For Excellence in Poetry.

Photo Credit: Denyse Coutu

Translators' Biographies

Sylvain Gallais is a native French speaker transplanted to the U.S. twenty years ago. He is an emeritus professor of Economics at Université Francois Rabelais (Tours, France) and of French in the School of International Letters and Culture at Arizona State University. His co-authored book in economics is entitled *France Encounters Globalization* (2003).

Cynthia Hogue's tenth collection of poetry, *instead, it is dark,* will be out in 2023. With Sylvain Gallais, she translated *Fortino Sámano (The overflowing of the poem),* from the French of Virginie Lalucq and Jean-Luc Nancy, which won the Landon Translation Award from the Academy of American Poets, and *Joan Darc,* by Natalie Quintane. Hogue's honors include two NEA Fellowships and the Witter Bynner Translation Fellowship. She is the inaugural Marshall Chair in Poetry Emerita Professor of English at Arizona State University.

Distantly
Nicole Brossard
Translated by Sylvain Gallais and Cynthia Hogue

Cover art: Cynthia E. Miller, born 1953, "New York, April, 2009,"
Acrylic paint with chalk pastels and oil paintstick on canvas 32" x 52"
Photographed by Tim Fuller, Private Collection Cemillerart.com

Typefaces: Garamond Premier Pro and Briem Script Std

Cover design by Adam Bonnanon
Interior design by Ken Keegan

Printed in the United States
by Books International, Dulles, Virginia
On 55# Glatfelter B19 Antique 360 ppi
Acid Free Archival Quality Recycled Paper

Publication of this book was made possible in part by gifts from
Katherine & John Gravendyk in honor of Hillary Gravendyk,
Francesca Bell, Mary Mackey, and The New Place Fund

Omnidawn Publishing
Oakland, California
Staff and Volunteers, Spring 2022
Rusty Morrison & Ken Keegan, senior editors & co-publishers
Laura Joakimson, production editor and poetry & fiction editor
Rob Hendricks, editor for *Omniverse* & fiction, & post-pub marketing
Sharon Zetter, poetry editor & book designer
Liza Flum, poetry editor
Matthew Bowie, poetry editor
Anthony Cody, poetry editor
Jason Bayani, poetry editor
Gail Aronson, fiction editor
Jennifer Metsker, marketing assistant